With deep sensibility and and honest poems consider medicinal properties of tra the world's sorrows. On a visit to Paris, the poet our privileged American life while viewing an exhibition by Syrian photographers: "a white-haired woman in the road kneels beside a bloodied child. the word for this woman is grandmother. is refugee." Maxson cautions we "must not acknowledge despair as a chemical component of this air we have no choice but to breathe...." Yet we are continually offered hope in her fierce belief in the beauty of the world. "They say," she writes, that the tears of a turtle "are never shed in grief but only as a physiological process, an excretion of sodium, & the butterfly's attendance/ only to some nourishment there & not a kiss upon that turtle's grief nor even/ the impulse to grace in such a kiss/ but only supply & demand. I disagree.... Sometimes what we perceive/ as the perfection of tenderness is just that."

—CAROL CIAVONNE,
editor of *Posit*, author of *Azimuth* and *Birdhouse Dialogues*

Maxson's movements are those of history, music, natural disasters, a heaving ocean, the "wind in pines," all of which, like her own thrilling grammar, are "not to be wrestled into sentences." Instead, like "subcontinental grinding plates," her lines carve out new and lasting forms. In this stunning collection, the poet makes space for us to contemplate a natural world that is bound for catastrophe and yet filled with breathtaking beauty. Her poems direct our gaze to the deer in the thicket, the moral certitude of a child, the Angelus Novus, hurtling (with us) forever forward.

—ELIZABETH MURPHY,
editor of Grid Books

Suzanne Maxson's poetry brings together great complexities of related ideas. Her poems rise from a particular topography, a tracing of paths, and of histories. She has an ear for the musical in language and an eye for its placement on the page.

—PAT NOLAN,
publisher, Nualláin House; poet and translator

These subtle and sophisticated poems invite us into the interior life of a shining intelligence. "I found my way slowly, distracted and absorbed by every beauty," Suzanne Maxson writes. The richness of her past infuses her present with a wry sadness, an awareness of loss balanced by an intricate perception of the living moment. "I suppose this is a prayer," she writes, "that every being ... be offered a night sky of stars...." Reading these poems, you are bound to see the night sky and the stars more precious and more clearly than you had before.

—ELIZABETH HERRON,
Sonoma County Poet Laureate,
author of *In the Cities of Sleep* and *Insistent Grace*

This polished, accomplished collection sings of living awake in this "unjust and violent world unfurling always into chaos." Deeply observed and wry, experience is simultaneously historical and cosmological, suffering both particular and global. Suzanne Maxson invites us to consider loss and the mind-stopping joys of art and connection through poems that are fresh and true. Reading them, I felt recognition and expansion, as I would after a nourishing conversation with a wise friend.

—VALERIE BREWSTER CALDWELL,
art director and book designer

Suzanne Maxson is enamored of beauty and of the mystery that radiates from even its slightest, most idiosyncratic manifestation. Seeing a Welsh farmer's crooked teeth, his "broken brown teeth," she urges us to keep "coming into mystery, choosing it." And in the title poem, we witness Helen Keller, deaf and blind from early childhood, learn finally at age 72 what the word "jump" means—in Martha Graham's studio, her hands on the waist of dancer Merce Cunningham: "and he jumped, rose up and her hands rose up with his body, again again again again ... oh she said oh how wonderful! how like thought!" Such brightness! Here is poetry that springs, that leaps like Merce Cunningham, like the mind of Helen Keller.

—LEE ROSSI,
author of *Wheelchair Samurai* and *Darwin's Garden*

MOVEMENT

Suzanne Maxson

I'm trying to figure out two very simple things:
how to live and how to die, period.
That's all I'm trying to do,
all day long.

—Maira Kalman

. . . and all that I beheld respired with inward meaning.

—William Wordsworth

Movement

Fernwood Press
Newberg, Oregon
www.fernwoodpress.com

Printed in the United States of America

Page design: Mareesa Fawver Moss
Cover art: Suzanne Maxson
Author photo: Izzi Lipari Maxson

ISBN 978-1-59498-115-9

For my family.

Contents

Gratitude

to my dharma guide and teacher Dan Jorgensen (1945-2020)
for those precious retreats

to Amanda Lipari Maxson, for loving poetry

to Karen Turner, Carol Ciavonne, Phil Forester,
Alan Porter, Paul Hoge, and Elizabeth Murphy

and still & always to Robert, for everything

Acknowledgments

"Art," "Southern Exposure," "All Right," "The Long Thought," "Chosen," "An Offering of Vowel Sounds," and "Questions Before Sleep About Iris Murdoch" appear in *Posit, a journal of literature and art*, September 2023; "After War" in *Reverberations: A Visual Conversation* (exhibition catalog); "Not a Place" as a limited edition broadside by North Bay Letterpress Arts.

Photographs by the author.

Notes

Poetry could be regarded as magical incantation, fundamentally a matter of sound and of the power of sound to bind our minds' and bodies' apprehensions within an acoustic complex. On the other hand, poetry is a matter of making wise and true meanings . . . A poet cannot bring us any truth without introducing into the poetry the problematic, the painful, the disorderly . . .

—Seamus Heaney in *The London Review of Books*, 1987

The universe, this external world, the seasons and eons
mere moments. Everything is impermanent. . . .
Life and breath are like lightning and dew.

—Jamgön Kongtrul, 1813-1899, tr. by Ken McLeod

Sentences

That habit. See the verb
   insisting & punctuation
as though by alien will arising, finding

a way in as though the universe being energy and mass
     , as though the universe, being energy
mass and vibration as it is compels rhythm, sound

     (and vibration, as it is) compels / determines
determines content and form. Likewise in the mind
       thought by alien will appears as sentences.

Evidence exists for: dark matter everywhere, ultimate
     emptiness recognizable & known
but this addiction to the sentence this illusion

of completion, an illusion of necessity—
       : Grateful as usual to the Buddhists
and the Physicists for their guidance but envious

of the Musicians
     this infinite topography
of light
     not to be wrestled into sentences

PLACEMENT

Backyard

Hillside, suppose, of oak.
creek run   watershed   time before
unrecognizable now in this small plot
a bungalow   some body's
            effort circa 1929, somebody's satisfaction
            somebody else's assumption of
                              responsibility for
                              this made place—

Between the hill & the lagoon suppose
a Pomo foot path. now pave it.
                                to town for pins
& ribbon at the five & dime. drug store. depot.
            all that business being somebody's effort
of belief, some body's day by day
                                     their season—

                                     Here still
his backyard path a proper curve, his rock wall, roses
            chosen for fire, poppies for black
every tree a gesture of his restless mind, a decision
                                              an addition
to the view, & subtraction—one tree down to favor another
envisioning grace   shade   color   all of it only
attitude—one morning complete
            satisfaction, perfection, tomorrow
a list of labors, occasion for despair.   now nostalgia—

See how in the photograph
            he was alive, you were a little girl
& the view   how in those days it opened all the way
through the backyards up the hill.
            & what's underground
            entangled in the fungal dark, suppose
                              his ultimate intimacy
with that   as mineral ash   in watershed

Not a Place

Begin in rock—
sedimentary sea floor uplifting
eroding   then subcontinental grinding plates
rafting coastal granite north to carve Bodega Bay
    and in the east arise volcanic cinder cones belching
        ash & lava   basalt   obsidian   pumice & tuff
    along an alluvial plain. Sonoma Mountain not a place
    but this movement
                    and in water—
wild ocean and into it Gualala, Pomo waters-coming-down
as Ashokawna   Russian River   Rio Ruso   & agua
    caliente underground,   numberless running creeks, tidal
    esteros, Petaluma slough   & on the plain these seasonal
        shifting marshes of Laguna de Santa Rosa
                        rising on the rains.
                                    or in the names—
Pomo   Wappo   Sotoyome   Miwok.   Tso-noma, where legend
sees the moon born.   in Kota'ti   Kalé   Pe'taluuma.
                                    Entonces llegan
Juan Francisco Bodega, Mariano Vallejo, Maria Carrillo.
        Aquí Santa Rosa de Lima.
    Now O'Farrell.   Guerne.   Heald.   Rohnert.   Dominion
    audibly arising & falling
    in the rhythms of naming
                        or in the work—
of fishers, hunters, basketmakers. of cattle ranchers
redwood loggers chicken farmers apple pickers. of stonemasons
mercantilers field hands profiteers. of raising up & ripping down.
of labor unnamed. refugees, immigrants, suburban settlers, utopian
    dreamers & the ones who made movies, made music, made defiant
    love & a little revolution in the woods. of a few beloved
    stubborn saviors of our rattled earth.
        of all those arriving   striving   dying
                                    disappearing en ondas.

Begin & end in a blue
salutatory sky— not a place but all this
movement   (call it history)   (call it time)

Yosemite

I.

The first long journey of John Muir
was a thousand miles on foot
to the Gulf of Mexico
with intention
to get to South America—a calling
to the tropical—but malaria took him
and then a ship to that summer
in the Sierra.

Understanding tides not only
as the pulse of nature
and of human affairs but as
the primal thing,
as life itself and so finding time
too precious to waste in the factory
he undertook to be carried along
on tidal longing.

I heard his words
at night in bed, his journal
along that purposeful endeavor.
What he saw!
The world God made! he said
every day offering up itself
as form and feeling always new to him
and beautiful.

I could not sleep.
Overcome by those Cumberland
Mountains where he awoke among
freshets and birdsong

and all the botanical and animal
variant wild, encountering also some
Kentuckians, my mind fell in love
with all of it.

My own longing
settled into the sound of his words
in which an alien and enviable
awareness
undertook in his time and placement
to find in ecstasy Yosemite, here
in this state where nightly I lie down,
California.

2.

He was moved
to the work of Thoreau
whom he admired extravagantly
regretting
that such a kindred soul never
walked on westward to the Sierra
to witness all that God
offered there.

Thoreau however
heeded a closer call, to the nearby
where he found abundant in his East
enough splendor
for the senses to apprehend. Anyway
as he died there quietly at forty-four
he said according to his sister Now
Comes Good Sailing.

What they shared
as I perceive it was a silence,
knowing that to go alone in silence
        to go lightly
is the only way to get into the heart
of it all, translating that stillness
and their restlessness
        into words.

I hear it,
continuing what must be my kind
of journey, through sleeplessness
        and longing
into days unfathomably
unlike mine, another lifetime
into this consuming gratitude
        for the words.

Paris: a travel guide

History: One day many years
      ago passed Susan Sontag on the street in Saint Germain
looking up into the sky   maybe the architecture   maybe
into a thought   her exhilaration still with me as the present
falls off onto the freeway to the airport causing a smash-up
that blocks all lanes north of the Golden Gate. That time ago
comme une ile flottante her face but too late for the riots of '68
too late for Alice & Gertrude, for de Beauvoir & Sartre
all that   too late   for the 19th century when Haussmann's
boulevards smashed medieval streets and a critic mourned
"the costly confusion, the triumphant
                    vulgarity, the awful materialism
we pass on to our descendants"   Now many years ago
il y a longtemps   les Arènes de Lutèce a rowdy Roman
entertainment, or before the Romans showed up & Celtic
Parisii rowed the Seine, the Marais a marsh   *il y a longtemps*
before the measure of years into cities ripe and overripe
with the living   where among the sapiens we trade
not in apparel & perfume but in the air itself, eager traders
in the treasure of breath.   until like stars we go out.

Why visit? It's a pilgrimage
      to Paris a city a street where we feasted on the confection
called *iles flottantes*. Now a face in that window, woman
in the glass, not quite visible seems definitely now to be
looking at me. possibly my mother has come to Paris.
Do the dead come to Paris? in my face? Do the old
come to Paris? Inhabiting every street. *well how did I get here?*
                    water flowing underground
Inexorable and holy this continuing on in age. the joyful
sigh.   this face a beginning   because he went out.
making an end.   *same as it ever was*
          les iles flottantes

What to see: Over an afternoon glass of rosé
in the Latin Quarter café   a bright hive, students
fiercely intimate her tangerine hijab & his superbe green
leather pointed shoes & noisy kids kick multilingual footballs
in the street after school, la république!   But read the news
through rosy glass of rage and desolation in the banlieues.
Tangentially   the memory of 1957
imprinted as a snapshot—tents laid down across the river
in Jordan, scales on the flesh of the earth & the word for this
was refugees.   is refugees.   In the exhibition
of Syrian photographers a thin boy naked legs red blanket
held to his heart, sleeping there between his parents'
fresh graves. next on the wall a white-haired woman
in the road kneels beside a bloodied child.   the word
for this woman is grandmother. is refugee. is a Syrian
grandmother now in French rain crossing the périphérique
far from Damascus.

Parisians: They sing
with abandon—bursting into song in a shop, confident
tenors in the bar with Charles Trenet, in the supermarket
harmonizing arm in arm, that long table at lunch bursting
into a medley & everybody knows the words, tre ragazzi
stomping down a passage sing big, in the jardin d'enfants
little voices under a window where Umm Kulthum overflows
somebody's heart & the Metro rappers & everywhere
this bursting bursting into song.

Packing light: In a rainy day
at the end of the Coulée Verte, beyond the périphérique
in the Buddhist temple the lama renowned for his singing
found woolly slippers for my wet feet and served us
Coca Cola. Form is not other than emptiness.
In this travelogue of pilgrimage, fact is not other than fiction
fiction not other than form. how Hemingway described
the supreme importance   of what's left out.
that the *dignity of movement* of an iceberg
is due to seven-eighths of it
being under the water.

Wars Begin Always in Beauty

From that city
by the bright sea under white sky
sweating in the back seat in 1957
in a hired car up the road
above that sea to Baalbek
to stand up straight for snapshots
in the ruin of fallen temples,
            an American child.

And along the road back
to that city, a shaded terrace
& three little boys bend over a game
with small stones, laughing in fractured light
bowls of white yogurt & grape leaf
& hookahs & Gauloises, men laughing
together. The black suits, the kaffiyeh
            her beautiful new shoes.

And in that city
Beirut on an evening sea
in the dining room the waiter bows
presenting a menu lettered in gold, heavy
as an atlas of the world.   Have the white fish
and dessert served by the waiter in white
is Peaches Melba—bright fruit, white plate
white cloth   sweet red sauce a blood-streak
and her father says Eat!   red the color
                        in something unseen.

Morning on the beach
wading into beauty into
stone-bright light, she can see
bottom, shining out beyond her depth   something
she wants to know, but he's waving his Time magazine
calling her back   from light too deep
                        to America.

My son, an American child has a question:
how the wars begin
We're eating our eggs
on toast in 1980, summer again
ruins, fractured light
in the names of God
an atlas of the world in the bright yolk a blood spot

what he wants to know. So tell my son
a story: Wars
begin always in beauty

that city burning now, the old sky
black by smoke, the water
black by blood, in this day
lost to that light but surely
not to beauty

The Conquest of Bread

In Ukraine the president's wife
mourns that her little son who once
loved to dance and play the piano
now wants only to be a soldier.

A farmer in Ukraine speaks
of a project to feed the people
in wartime, providing free grain
to the granaries who freely

will grind it for the bakers
to freely bake the bread, thus
providing that sustenance
to the people, who in Ukraine

sometimes at home speak Russian.
The Russian Pyotr Kropotkin dreamed
of providing to all people good health
and bread and happiness, proclaiming

to the twentieth century and to this one
the dangers in devotion to capital
and in resignation to the cruelties
of greed. He dreamed

that pianists might sometimes work
with a collective of carpenters, each
engaged in the skills and the pleasures
of their work, thereby

fulfilling each in a meaningful life
and providing the people with music.
In Ukraine the people did sing
in the early days of this war

in basement shelters, and even
between bombings brought pianos
into the public squares where also
elderly women learned to shoot.

Kropotkin observed in the lives
of animals that their survival
is not bound in competition
but in mutual aid, in cooperation

and even in mutual pleasure, as birds
take flight together in the joy of it.
Neither Adam Smith nor Darwin
took sufficient notice of generosity

and joy. Kropotkin also, in his
observations, understood empathy
as a quality neither universally
nor uniquely human.

In everything exists the possibility
for generosity. Kropotkin's dream
endures in the farmer's project
offering bread.

As for survival, witness also
the intelligence of the slime mold
in whom singular and plural
are permeable states:

in challenging conditions
the membranes of those single cells
will fuse in a protoplasmic collectivity
of response, rising

to that challenge in movement
of primordial elegance. The wisdom
of slime molds does not now preoccupy
the citizens of Ukraine

but Kropotkin might recognize in it
The Conquest of Bread, his manifesto
for that utopian dream of the collective
as we might see

from the heights of time like birds
all human history as movement
in a protoplasmic migratory waltz.
The soldier dreams of dancing.

The farmer dreams of bees.
In her dream an old woman
lifts a rifle and wishes to awaken
in her bed. The carpenters sing.

The citizens in our dreams
are birds, soaring above borders
in liberation from the cage of nations
where presidents dream their dreams.

Al Sur: Manifest Destiny

She feeds on words, peels away
meaning
          to sniff & chew
on the sound:

"I hate to see them suffer" he said.

Suffer.
a flower, growing wild
by roadsides in Kentucky
and neighboring states.
Something like sweetpea
but larger, the color of cream, fragrant
of vanilla, like the bean.

∞

Said he hates to see suffering.

hollow flaky pastry,
round, like a creampuff, but fried
in hot grease so it crunches. a suffering.

Something fragrant. Tasty.

∞

In the wind nothing
moves
but the wind. Everything else
is evidence only, clues
to what no creature sees—except

maybe bats, in their way, and they
only at night.

everything bending
but it's only—she knows
by the sound—the wind.

∞

Suffers in the café
from the salmon. overcooked.
Opens a notebook to write
about food, the weather,
the beetle on the windowsill

like the shell of a sunflower seed. unsalted.

∞

Says he hates to see suffering.
She contemplates the taste.

∞

She's reading the news, reading
about trouble in a country
with a musical name.

Some Ways a Day Begins

            /Garbage truck
6 a.m. rattling her skull, rolling it over
& up for the morning shift again but lately
so hard, that step into her shoes to do it
            again.   /The sight
of your red-haired neighbor alone in the green boat again
into the black water as she rows alone now   every morning
right on time at 7 o'clock rain or shine.   /After a long night
            the baby's awake
again so which of them will haul their body up into the cold
again and bring him to their bed for the morning feast
on every kind of sweetness still miraculous.
            /Alien dawn
penetrating this purgatorial tent where he fled
from calamity leaving everything   leaving nothing now
that everything is lost and he awoke knowing that not today
nor any other day will his sleeping children awaken at home.
            /A fortunate hour
for morning tea   to notice how windowlight enters
variously into their heart   into their living hands
into my eyes.   /Familiar thud, they're bombing again
            but this bomb
exploding the wall and the baby in her cot
beside that wall before it happened, before the scream
that rose in the throat and never will be gone
            from every morning.

The Arithmetic

Arrived as black mold, metastasized
as *not enough* for rent to keep 2 rooms
    & brown birds in a bush outside
    the window chirping & next door
    that saxophone in the afternoon
until eviction. sleeping cold in the car
in a dead end but anyway the car
until the fire.
    Penalties with interest compounded
    now for every loss but anyway
    complete the paperwork.
        In the dirt camp
here under the bridge we do what we can
to remember what's holy, to safeguard
the heart but every day an arithmetic
of minus. washing blistered infected feet
in a public sink   this is not   this is
    my life.   remember like light
    a door   a table   a bed
    flickers that light like a movie   without sound
no ticket to get back in. remember me   I remember
the painted table in that light   sufficient
even minus the saxophone

Placement

from Ruby Prudence

Little Ruby five years old
says *Nonna, nothing's perfect!*—her stern gaze
a caution, the wise child's first philosophical
certainty—when I say it's perfect, this home

this garden where Ruby can wander
on little feet among the trees and stones,
perfection despite of necessity now being
a Land-Lady (from Old English *hlafdie*,

loaf-maker, house-holder, a woman
of superior position assigned by ownership
of the land—all apply) of this particular dirt,
and with the many in need of home

exchanging shelter, comfort, even beauty
for rent, two lives finding
our requirements for security
met in relativity—Land-Lady and Tenant

our placements assigned
by biography   understanding
in this undeniable inequity
Ruby's admonition.

Arranging their placements,
Ruby among her dolls
speaks her thoughts in their languages
explaining the situation.

Good Fortune

From what does hope arise
for those who live on the inland flat
no hilltop horizon to move the eye
upward, no radiant amber remainder
of autumn lit now by that fractional ray
& visible there on the rise
    one   yellow   tree
in clean air   in this fortunate landscape
on the marginal shore
of a desperate nation?
imagination maybe.   lies.   the lotto.
history vivid as mirage.   or a prairie sky
comprehended as heaven.   somehow it does.

The Shoes in My Closet

Earliest humans did not wear shoes
but soon they fashioned shoes
from hides or reeds, protection
from some weather or terrain,
and soon, as boots or sandals,
in an ornamental expression
of caste or taste.
Is it right that I own these many shoes
for every possible weather, work,
or celebration, while so many
have no shoes?

The Grandmother's House

Remember when
in California bungalows
a tiny doweled window high
in a bedroom closet invited air
            and light into long dresses
and at that time God entered also as dust
lit by sun through Venetian blinds & devotion
to the Virgin flickered in ruby glass

while a child in her contentment wondered
about nothing but another mudpie
and what creamy darkness
            in this morning's mud
and even better why not add that rose-
scented lotion in Grandma's musty cupboard
and the rosebud cap to top off the pie

No rose lotion now but another stucco
bungalow, no ruby glass no candle here
for the Virgin but Avalokiteshvara
            No little window for light
in my closet, no dresses, these girls
untutored in solitude but content in this
known architecture, their Nonna's house

in an apocalyptic epoch   in the tidal presence
of solid objects in cupboards & drawers
dust in slanting light still *de spiritu sancto*
            where in the afternoon
behind the curtain into my closet
they make tea parties
and might remember

Morning in the Gallery

The frame a picture frame
wherein a grandmother has juxtaposed
two watercolors
for their virid green, their complicated
yellow and some colors of stonefruit
in paint laid down by her son, age eleven
and his daughter, a young woman
but the the tissue of time now
dissolves
into the same translucent hues, kinship
in color and the movement of brushes
as an old lady awakens at 7 a.m.
into generations.

The frame a rectangle of windowglass
and through the open arch of a painted wall
appears the silver-mottled column of the birch
already shedding leaves not even halfway
to Solstice,
and across the steep street a neighbor's
Heavenly Bamboo apparently on fire
every morning, set alight by the sun
through this bright summer fog
and the print edition of the news
in its blue wrapper still on the porch
where little Annie
will never again be seen because quietly
she died on the day before yesterday,
seventeen years a good span for a dog
but not much consolation in that for each
who loved her
enacting now behind that door the insufficient
rituals of loss with her little bed her toys her bowl
her collar with the flower made of cloth, just as

we perform them
for all the lost beloveds, the bed too big
the sweaters the shoes in the closet.
But do not allow
that absence into the frame.
Grief will not fit.

The frame this yellowed brittle page
of a paperback purchased in 1966 called
The Words
by Jean-Paul Sartre where the memorable
sentence recollected is still there underlined
and starred although he confesses that
"what I have written is false. True. Neither
true nor false."

(Describe in words as a conscious gaze framing
the presence of the moment and of the past
what is only, really, a blank stare, the brain
struggling to comprehend life in daylight.
false. True. Neither)

Do not allow absence into the frame. Today
do not allow grief

The frame a flat screen. catastrophe.
catastrophe. Again today catastrophe, brutality.
Briefly the president the general the journalist
the analyst the publicist the scientist but absent
the poet of catastrophe.

The frame a black cavern of bone
where Grandmother Spider spins her thread
of consciousness. She will not stop
spinning the senses into perception
to be named.

What I have written is neither true nor false.

Conversation Overheard on the Ferry

It rumbles & lurches.
The little boy's nervous.
The woman
    grandmother maybe
holds him closer, says

It's just the water moving.
        —Moving itself?
            (a serious question)
The water's always moving.
        —Is it moving itself?

He's waiting. I listen. She answers

It moves like we all do.
    The ocean is a body moving.

He's silent, satisfied.
            Then she says

The stagnant pool is a breeding place
                for disease

and we rumble across the strait
            into her mind.

Mountaineers

for Gabriel

What they brought fit
into the car: her body
knotted by some unremembered
story, the body of a child becoming
other, absent body of another child
& holy longing   for the innocence born
into this history she made for them
in this world that made us, the fathers
& all the undrawn maps we study
at night   all hauled on vacation
to see how it is at this elevation

because travel
is to see how that baggage will suit
a new landscape   how a body settles
into another air, what shadow
it makes from new light, how it walks
on this dirt   to discover
a single small white cotton sock
behind a rock   climb a boulder
glacier-carved to be conquered
by summer children unmindful
of time, although
their fretful mothers fit them into it
again every morning
like shoes.

Out on the lake
in a green canoe
not a boy, not a man
but a dreaming passage, out there
en route, entering emptiness
to understand what fills it.

Home Movie

for Roxy

In a winter noon
a family   in scenes
scripted from stories:
See 3 boys cooking pudding
at thirty frames per second.

Do we recognize fire
only because it burns
in the fire-place? China
just a name for those
bowed mountains under a sky
colored yellow in the painting?

See this tenderness.
at the window one
gazing. one bringing a bowl
to the table. one

with a secret, arranging
a tea set for the offering of milk
to soft animals, an offering
of devotion to every animal.
mine the soft cheeks
of a princess in sleep   she
whispers now, awakening

Siblings

20th C. usage through anthropology and genetics,
from Old English sibb *(kinship, relationship, familial love)*
through Middle English compounds of sib
encompassing love and concord.
Proto-Germanic sibja—*(blood relation, properly "one's own")*
and the Indo-European root *swe *(self).*

Of a solitary childhood, lacking
sisters or brothers to awaken
every morning with the same

parents—however present or absent
harrowing or temporary those might be—
but waking always
as the only,

and solitude being the ordinary condition,
unworthy of much attention, and memory
dependent upon the light of attention,

the synapse opens often on long moments
of solemn conjugation,
the inconstant body reaching

into intimacy, knowing
of a sudden one's own blood
in the other

kinship discovered
encompassing love

Natural History

A bird was making its nest.
In the dream, I watched it closely:
in my life, I was trying to be
a witness not a theorist.
—Louise Glück

Something I missed:
not enough with the wild
& thus I live in shame.

Hummingbird why
do I not know your tongue
your tiny heart? Where
do the squirrels go
to die? So many born
into this garden then
vanishing. Today awoke
still in the strong dream
of a deer at the end
of her natural life
in her natural death
in a thicket, not a car in sight.

Alone but never
alone at dawn at high altitude
on a mountain lake to know
those colors. Never dared
the trail. Never studied
species as they live, never
spent days in contemplation
of theirs. No spring pilgrimage
to desert wildflowers, too lazy
to drive thirty minutes
to the coast where I do not
find as many people do
solace, gritty sand in my ears

on a windy beach—but why
not even the peace of a canoe
on an estuary, blissfully
to know the dark water
that way? And entering
on skis a vast empty white
expanse of silent snow, never.
I'm sunk in shame.

Once long ago
pulled over on Highway 1
at no place particular
to lie down, ear to the dry dirt
desperate to hear the earth
humming. Briefly have ventured
to the granite scarps and bright
tidal pools, known silence
in a cool mossy grove, rested
in the yellows of a meadow
while the advisory voice
in my head said *now here*
you are! in this natural world

but even trees, you
who are gods to me, you
whom I know to be
in your underworld
of infinite interdependence
our teachers, even you
I fail to witness by name
which, although it's nothing
to you, is careless, disrespectful
on my part

and reading the words
of those who know
what I do not know and
how to say it, what I feel
is admiration, then
gratitude, then shame
and also envy. And grief
of course because
these days it all translates
as grief, as knowledge
of what will be lost.

The Physical Universe

Sounds like middle C in the midrange
plus some funk in the woofer —Gabe Maxson

Here it is. Gravity—lacking
in the discourse but here
in the physical universe where apples fall
    on earth always downward

where somebody might be falling
falling hard when he tries to get up
    cross a room, be somewhere
    not the chair—down & down
feeling that funk in the woofer, & here

where in the end we go to ground
or ashes & even the visible distant sky suggested
universal gravitation   now we know   it's in waves.
fifty times more energy than all the stars   rippling
    the fabric of spacetime! Einstein getting it right again

in 1915 & here it is, gravity   holding me
down on the couch, sending tree limbs down
after the rain. the rain. rockets that fail to exit fall back
    to earth. tears drain downward   leave a track of salt

these waves detected at last by an interferometer laser
their signals simulated as sound vibrations audible
    to human ears, little ears on earth
where we live awash in these waves

of middle C soothing
in the midrange, of inevitable funk in the woofer

An Offering of Vowel Sounds

According to a white-haired writer
the musician has notes for making music but the poet
has vowels. think about wind in Japanese maples.
thinking to read this book under my crooked hand
about the soul of an octopus but unable.
to read. lacking concentration thinking
one summer on the Strait, practicing departure
as line breaks, feeling for the first time movement
as wind in pines undertaking perfection
as a celadon Hermes 3000 typewriter
in a battered VW van, campground
on the water, a cushion, a mug

Now move some furniture. Carry a painting
to this wall from that one, table better there
than here, lamp four inches farther left on that table
now get up and move it back again to get it
right, precisely. thereby disturbing little dog
at rest. all this compulsive up & down
a seasonal weeding out
out out of mental disorder.
But I do have vowels. In the subjectivity
of the vowel sound, assonance
might open like a state of grace.

Every death a disappearance into bone or shell
& what to make of it. Make home
in memoriam of those
disappeared into these
objects of beauty and devotion.
into photographs (the camera
re-engineered our experience of death. of life)

But equally floats this home on joyful motion
as a Tibetan prayer begins
Having obtained this excellent free and well-favored life
and it is
and in vowel sounds I call out to my children
Here I am for you, imperfect
but present into the future
which already is here

NOT THE END OF THE WORLD

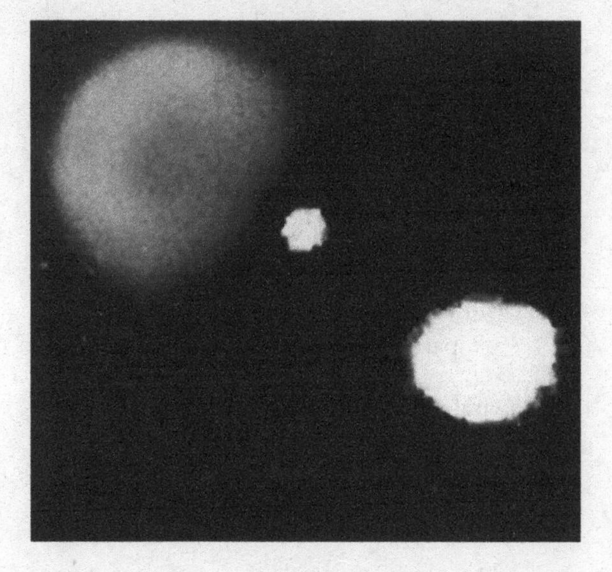

Everything falls away from us—
the light, the dark, the warm afternoons—and all we can do
is cry out in affirmation of our joy.
—Pico Iyer

Leap Year

Pandemic fear
of the virion. Fire & fear
of fire. Fear of rising tides
of fear itself, captivity
under the red dawn even
on the green lagoon.
                                        Red sky
at morning, sailors take warning—
all of us mariners now on this ocean
of uncertainty & danger, crowded boats
capsizing all around us in the maelstrom
and rats
        in the dark below deck.

In a burnt world what will become of you
who own no doors & windows, no machines
to clean your only air, not even a certified
        particle-filtering mask

In a viral wind will I welcome you
into the safety of my solitude, take you
into my arms to share this shelter,
        will I

and what comfort to offer
to the children of our children?
On earth we have arrived into
        these questions

Not the End of the World

Because it was Wednesday, took a dogwalking detour
for curbside pickup from the pottery shop of the plates
painted on our good-bye day by my granddaughter & me
        in nostalgia for her childhood
but it was closed—an annoyance because it was late
in the day for a walk & already hot & I wanted
to see the colors made by firing
                as she entered her future.

What day it is a question
        in 2020. Turns out
        was Tuesday (always closed)

On Wednesday: apocalypse
we say
        nuclear winter, say
the sky's not right

8 a.m. black
& vermilion (from childhood a favorite
                of the infinite colors
which recently I learned
                is cinnabar, & toxic)
we awakened apparently
        on Mars or maybe in Hell

Meteorologically there is
a reason why. wild fires. smoke shooting into the upper atmosphere
        over hundreds of miles, absorbing the blue light we see
        as sky, allowing only red-orange-yellow into our eyes
Historically also
reasons.   First Industrial Revolution
        Second Industrial Revolution
        Consequences

now rendered silently in such dark beauty
despite signs & warnings & incontrovertible
data
into the visible spectrum at dawn

and I must not acknowledge despair
as a chemical component of this air we have
no choice but to breathe
because the grandchildren
cannot bear that

Clearance

The fragile ash has landed
bearing a message
                                        from what it was
charred newsprint bearing words still
visible, announcing a sale at Ace Hardware
on garden tools, and so to that neighborhood
                                                    to those neighbors
                                                              good-bye
and in blackened leaves still recognizable
as oak & bay, so to that woodland east
of the river beyond the cultivated rows
goodbye   Possum deer raccoon human
            refugees now, or consumed in what ruin
they clung to at that   moment   Tender ash
floating like snow, white
                                                    clean as snow
on magnolia maple ferns remaining
after evacuation to await
                                                    the vegetal quiet.
Good-bye or maybe for the lucky
only à bientôt when again   again
reminded to remain in uncertainty we return
to hummingbirds still outside the window
& unpack treasures back into their places, pray
thanks again that not yet   have these faces
these words been lifted up
                                                    as ash
to bear a message from what this was

A Simple Familiar Question, as Intended

How are you? how
are you doing?   Intended second person
singular directed to oneself, a simple familiar
question as intended but now,now—this word

demanding repetition now,
our white cane tapping to remind us
where we are—experienced now
experienced as a complicated riddle. So

give it a minute first to determine the current
condition, the strength of current
passing now through the body, determined
by sleep or lack of it, by news most recently

consumed, by an unwise helping
of sugar at breakfast, the reassuring
text message or lack of it, or failing
an accurate measure of that current, give it

another minute to recalibrate the pronoun
to something inescapably larger, a collective
condition. Remain silent considering
the we as we who abide here in this

capsule of white sweet-scented air
this blue-sky life these good neighbors, nobody
dying here today but doing fine, doing well
the anticipated answer but inadequate

to the scope of we who, plural and
collective, abide in these times. The riddle
now impossibly complicated. So give it
another minute but the pause becomes

awkward as one mutters to fill it, something
about the children, the food queues
the lonely death, the vast & bottomless
injustice and cruelty, the chokehold

witnessed in somebody's neighborhood
who cannot breathe. How are we
to save one another, how are we
to do what must be done? Maybe say

Could be better.

The President

According to the observing mind this thought now this one
compelling me into another another another & the deep
Devonian shale are equally ephemeral
that wasp among blossoms
& a star we think ten thousand million years ago equally
fleeting & the essential suffering of all beings apparent even

in that icteric eye, in that flesh a color I should call saffron
because in his essence *even that one* is like the monk
a difference only of conditions, all of us aching
from impermanence, some way suffering
in doubt, decay, the rage of fear, the poison
fruit of cruelty all around the cold cot of an infant
when the first thoughts formed. But it's insufficient
only to know

that even he who summoned an eyeless posse
to the demon realm of his ordinal Ignorance even that one
is lost in fear & longing
because as a crazing prospect that shatters the observing mind
arose this ephemeron, corrupting every next thought, afflicting
all sensibility, inflaming the open wounds of all who suffer now
now in this world. this one

Janus 1, past

OPEN they cry out now, demanding
signs in capital letters OPEN we are
open open for business   for your pleasure
for every face beloved   disdained or feared
to be naked and visible to be open as before

as before   as before downtown emptied into these
distances of meters or feet   longing   that children
again crowd into their schoolrooms not like now
in the family flat each at the end of their own
thin rope   or in the fields & factories needing

a clean breath   laboring still   for us   or some
wanting a late night at the bar comfortably drunk
or dancing in the hot breath of a crowd at the club
or alone maybe forever now   longing only
for the near breath   touch   of someone beloved

while the nurses & doctors reborn now
as our kachinas   bend into their dance of despair
and grief.   In the old language no such word
as covid   corona the ring of light
around the sun   and they want that   the past

Janus 2, future

Expressed as a grammar, future tense
simple we will live / will not live
or tense progressive will be living in / not
living in the unknown / unknowable

new year, less than this Leap Year by
just one day according to that artifact
of human calculation the calendar
its days & hours equal in number

to seventy-five percent of all years
or finding both grammars & numbers
unhelpful, predict the same old hopes
& longing / familiar fears & dread

for the better / of the worse
or picture Angelus Novus, that angel
of history who gazing at the wreckage
of the past would make whole

what has been smashed but instead
as the philosopher observed the storm
propels him into the future
to which his back is turned

where inevitably & despite
grammars calculations predictions
we must arrive with naked arms
like wings outstretched in prayer

May all beings enjoy happiness
May they be free from suffering
May they not be separate from true joy
May they rest in equanimity

Autobionomy

Dreamed a new body, its form
    a circle, hooped, an effort
of artifice.   In it   becoming it
from within   became freedom
to move through this infernal
air and into it   circling   came everything
we ever had been
            we   meaning I   meaning
two, meaning marriage, meaning
two and two and two into familias, meaning all
earthborn, everything ever we have known
as language or image now finding
new form, this hoop of memory
                As we gathered
at the border crossings, as we lay down
together in our coverlet of dust, as we sat
with the scraps spread before us and a bottle of glue
to labor as makers   awakening into this infected
weather. The bone heads we beat
                    against that Wall
                        broke upon that Wall.

Now a new body insensible
to weather   invulnerable to walls
made in   memoria
            dhakira
lifting now into this hot new air

Brokedown

from Walter Benjamin & Jordan Peele

1.

In the brokedown refrigerator
dank water pooled in the bin, bean soup grew mold
& wasted into its nature
but a sturdy second-hand replacement arrived a.m.
now in sweet company
with the dear old stove, all this white, this gleaming
so clean, so excellently
organized for bottles, butter, eggs, a yellow bowl.

2.

High noon has come
in other languages when the time for dread was finished.
We're in it now, say it
or don't: tanks in rows invisible but arriven, the new regime.
brown-eyed babies ripped
from the arms of mothers in your neighborhood right now.
hate-tainted scum bubbling
through cracks in every street from an underworld where
35% of every Western nation
cooks it up in kitchen pots but some blessed still believe
in elections. our ocean
a widening gyre composed of plastic, 2xTexas   and only
the Angel of History sees it all
wreckage upon wreckage   into the future   one single catastrophe

3.

After midnight now, little dog
& says here the poet carried his dying wife in late days
to the commode (he calls it)
holding her frail bones over it and then back to their bed
where her fingers fretted
at something (invisible to him) in the air.   impossible to know
what that was. my beloved
no longer beside me in our bed & drugged into some comfort
would anyway be deaf
to this night report, like you little dog beside me snoring
the goddamned world arriving
the damned arriven   beyond this bed   into the sunken place

Between

The only difference
between
is breath. we listen
for reassurance
in the steady breath
of the baby in her crib
breathe along
with the dear dog beside us
to comprehend
her consciousness
breathe the last
breath of the beloved
into our own lungs
knowing only then that it has gone
from them just as I did hold his
in mine
and just as the breath
of the Black man
on the asphalt
willfully was crushed in him
before our eyes & gone
from him
forever in that
instant
between

Sutra for 300 Days

Not here. not here. not here. not his breathing.
no breath. not his skin as I knew it, not his skin
though I feel it. not his shoulder, not his skin.
not the bones, even in dreams no bones. no feet
not his feet, not his two feet, the shuffle of his feet.
not his long hands. we weep but gone his fine hands.
not here. not here. not his body. not here, nowhere.
not his deaf ears. not his falling. not his losses.
not his words, no throat. not his anger, not here
nowhere. not his numbers. his counting. his doubt.
oh not his sighs, not even in dreams, his sighs only
ashes in my throat. not his piss. not his tears. not here.
no form no emptiness. no eye no ear no tongue
no mind consciousness om paragate parasamgate
not his body, that body parasamgate and his heart
not his heart. not his voice. not even his voice.
not his absence.   not his absence.   his absence

In Extremis

Dropping like flies not quite
the right expression to describe
how the beloveds go   one
by one   but something we say.

Do those flies left lingering attend
each inevitable ending in muscid grief
visible only to the compound eye?
that inevitability ≠ willingness

to drop & dry up on a windowsill
six legs rigid in air, blown down
on a draft or some rough simile
for what happens it seems

so often lately.   nothing lasts
long. nothing lasts long. nothing
lasts long.   that old Lakota song.
Good-bye & again good-bye to them

tucked into flannel on a downy bed
them tied by tubes to the breathing
machine or crumpled in a gutter in that
frigid drunken night & good-bye also

to them equally beloved but untimely
shot, choked, on asphalt shattered
under a boot, or sick & shooting up
in the toilet, to them who fled for refuge

into a rickety boat only to drown
brought down in the net we call borders
Farewell to each & all obliterated now by
mistake, under the delicate drone

Apologies my darling for this
obsession with endings, but how
can it be otherwise as we do fall
like the silver flies, one by one

Meanwhile however in love we feed
one another on deliciousness. also
that moment on the valley road when
an unexpected brightness pours out

from what had been horizon
as choral joy. & remember the end
of that Lakota song: only the earth
only the earth & the mountain

The Tangibles

for Kathy Kettler

The dead, according to some
perceptions, live in vivid afterlife
        until no one is left who knew them
                tangibly, then live on still
in a long thinning shadow until no one left alive
                        remembers that name.

Objects also, the treasures
gathered into a life, each
having its place in that life, containing afterlives
or the vision of a maker   the affection of a giver
or that gasp of desire that brought it home,   each
somehow   having become worthy of its place.
They testify
            that the past is not imaginary

and someday some might be
treasured equally by someone who understood
                        the soul made tangible there,
some discovered with delight at the yard sale
and offered an afterlife. Some end broken in the bin.
We write our wills and testaments pretending
it's our business to know but in the end we let go
                            one way or another

        meanwhile managing the tangibles
as masters of tidying-up   as practitioners
of Swedish death-cleaning or as anxious
hoarders   and even the old man homeless
for eighteen years found in the camp with only
a black plastic garbage bag
carried some treasure there
                        and let it go.

Mine are many and lately, of sudden
necessity living at the pace of   in the spirit
                                                            of the snail
in a surfeit of hours for reverie,
                                        like the snail's eyes
mine are feelers, locating each tangible
presence, practicing hello again
rehearsing good-bye.

Preparedness Manual

A way to prepare: behind glass doors
tied shut with ribbon see the coffee set
mid-century modern, my mother's (who
drank her coffee from a mug) now mine
(who never offered fancy service to a guest)
edges all unchipped, still pristine—imagine
the earthquake that will pop those doors
and there goes the coffee set—shards! nothing
lasts long.   might as well untie the ribbon.

But when ivy overruns the dryrock wall
and the stucco, when windowsills succumb
to wood rot, imagine thirty years untended,
that garden shovel buried under layers
(and does it matter why and how this happens
not by destruction but in absence and neglect,
happens even here in our clean town where
even now the asphalt cracks & crumbles?)
and practice maintenance.

Or fire: how these California seasons seem
to leave nothing but chimneys & ash & grief
but look—no need to imagine the new green
nor hope for wildflowers from the char because
behold: even where the black tree fell, here
is every color all still visibly undeniably alive
to the naked eye, and to witness this is equally
a way to prepare, one among the many as we
bask in pleasures of another day, prepared.

Questions Before Sleep About Iris Murdoch

To pierce the veil of selfish consciousness
and enter the world as it really is—this *unselfing*
she described as an effort of goodness, and art
as an occasion for that release
                    into the world as it is
and wrote that the essence of art is love
in its many dimensions, and that love, like art
                    is the discovery of reality.

It's possible I have her thinking wrong.
I encountered her words in a casual way
and not from careful reading of her work
but I wrote this down and I wonder now

about her last years
how that unselfing we call dementia
changed her mind. No effort of goodness in it, no art.
Did she pierce the veil of selfish consciousness?
Did she enter the world as it really is
or was it lost to her?
And love?

The Long Thought

The neuroscientists
located some places in the brain, a network
where apparently the catalog we call *myself*
lights up their brain-screens when intention takes a break—
posterior cingulate cortex, medial prefrontal cortex
constructing the long thought called *myself. I am*
I am the person who

mother and child, my tentative hand
on the flesh of her arm, wishing to be beside her on the couch
but reaching for the ashtray she swats it away, and cruelly
I reduced her character to this, although that body
contained complexities not manifest in photographs
now confused with her stories, her stories with the catalog
of memory & with those stories wherein I wrote her life
as fiction in an effort to decipher the single remaining snapshot
2x2 inches & blurred of a little girl, short bob & bangs
as that mother. And all along she was? In her body surely
and in mine now as shadow, developing sometimes into presence
as the photograph once developed in its chemical bath (which
is a way to explain one effect

of aging and its ailments)
or of another moment only her words, no photograph
but which I remember as a photograph: on a park bench
holding the hand of a tiny girl wearing a brown coat
and a bonnet, whose white shoes/red shoes dangled.
and her first intention

to leave that child on the bench

but how she held on, clutching (my word) the little hand
(my hand) unable to let it go, and then the second intention.
but a timely rescue. The doctor diagnosed a suicidal mood.
Hysterectomy might open a mood like a wound. Bonnet
brown coat red shoes probably my embellishment. That she
clutched the little hand my embellishment, an effort
to understand. Park bench? Possibly all embellishment
of a fractured remark as she wandered in the urgency
of language vanishing into the factual tumor
as the long thought called Ruth
came to an end, entering mine.

What She Said

Her cheeks rounded out in the smooth
steroidal approximation of a baby's
after years without & without, yearning
to die, the unwelcome will to live still
bucked her desire. Her thoughts
are not to be known but I will write
what she said in her immobile home
where in memory the carpet is blue although
that's not right and the walls reek as forever
of cigarettes, rental deathbed with a view
of the concrete carport and I wondered why not
in the room with a window on nesting quail
the California species separated in the Pliocene
from its relatives? She wanted to be closer
to the TV. When it happened I had wandered
outside for the mail and she was in herself
alone, as though she waited there within
to be alone again. But it must have been
some days before, and as I recall in a daylight hour
after conscientious drops of morphine under the tongue
not too much and not too little   that she whispered
lifted her eyes to whisper   *This dying*
takes a long time.

no pain
no yearning
no reaching
no turning
no heat
no need
no leaving
no breath

Maps

In a quiet room
still warm
his body

When I was six
& chopped my thumb cutting rope
with an ax, who put the bandage on

Who showed me the maps, named oceans
more real to him than the pansies
we planted   real as that ax

Who bought the bike to set me free
Who in the city said to me You drive that car
like it's part of you (that engine always in me)

At last to stand behind him, mapping
the pores & creases in his scalp as in his heart
he charted the Strait of Juan de Fuca

Who in the quiet room was gone
from the body but I fell on the clean
white feet, the freckled hands, and kissed each

Our geography
so quickly finished

Urgency

An itch as a phenomenon is always
urgent & if you scratch it another arises
of pleasure, and that itch recedes, evaporates   and if
you don't scratch that itch yes it evaporates—just after
the moment when you forget   to think it never will

or an ordinary nausea, longer arising
into sweat, the urgency of vomiting
longer to recede but with medicine
or without it that misery will end & again you'll know
the amazing grace   in the pleasure of food

or sometimes an urgent & terrible
longing   for someone gone from this tangible matter
might be relieved by tears or gardening, might
not, might respond to a stiff dose of something or not but you know
it will recede, evaporate into the absence of itself   just as he did

and the Anthropocene, this long
phenomenon arising in response
to human dominance as carbon heat
in oceans churning plastic & radioactive
garbage, even the deepest currents warming, veering
in new directions, melting old ice, and on land now floods & fires
famine & grief as human greed leaves its stain in the earth itself all this
until it recedes into another age unnameable
in these languages.   Neither we nor the grandchildren
nor theirs will be around to see how that goes
but like the rest it will go.

Ave

No landing without flight
No place the only place
No morning without a lifetime
            learning to awaken
from the comfort of night

Small birds return again
not minding that their names
remain unknown again
            every year, only
the crow known by name

A garden will sleep in frost
to awaken again always even
without the botanist without
            the ornithologist
to remember the names

No landing without the leap
No name for the leaping

MEDICINAL PROPERTIES

The transformation of the heart is a wondrous thing,
no matter how you land there. —Patti Smith

Movement

Helen Keller came to the studio
of Martha Graham. She felt the dancing
through the floor. But then a question:

What is jumping? I don't understand.
So Martha Graham led her to the barre
and said to the dancer Merce Cunningham

Merce, be very careful. I'm putting Helen's hands
on your body, and she did, Helen's hands
on his waist, at the barre, and he jumped—

in the studio no one moved, attending.

her hands, he said, like bird wings, so soft

and he jumped, rose up and her hands
rose up with his body, again again again again
and he felt her fingers moving as though fluttering

and when he stopped oh
she said oh how wonderful! how like thought!
how like the mind it is!

the choreographer, the dancer
and Keller at seventy-two the dance itself.
and how like the mind to leap

to John Cage, the music. and to that love

awakening silently, suddenly, as it does.

—from Craig Brown, Hello Goodbye Hello

Chosen

Choosing to settle in mystery which is
preferable in any morning to the news

as good fortune gave me senses
and time to read & contemplate

that in the Peruvian Amazon for example
& elsewhere, a butterfly feeds on the tears

of a turtle. Those tears they say
are never shed in grief but only

as a physiological process, an excretion
of sodium, & the butterfly's attendance

only to some nourishment there & not
a kiss upon that turtle's grief nor even

the impulse to grace in such a kiss
but only supply & demand. I disagree.

Capitalism never satisfies and Darwin
only partly. Sometimes what we perceive

as the perfection of tenderness is just
that, presenting itself to perception

just as in Wales we met an old farmer
blessed by crooked teeth untouched

by any dentist, & love for these broken
brown teeth arose like love for all

we call human, the unAmerican
imperfection of his teeth, their beauty

beyond reason, arising still in dreams
as the meaning of life. So you see

how it is, the geography in all of it
& the shock of benevolence & how

we come to a kind of settlement
with what we have allowed

into understanding, how we keep on
coming into mystery, choosing it

Jesus Sees Me Sleeping

His eyes I saw
from under the covers
in Grandma's bed
opening, and Jesus
did see me.

Later I learned
that an artist
created this effect,
but the child didn't know
about art.

Rothko

Paint.   a rectangle laid with color & floating over it
other colors. It may look simple he said
but it's got to be right.   calibration
of the edge not as division but quantum expansion
begun in the comfort of form, feeling it   open
                                        until light
entered, as it had done for others. thus, pilgrimage
into the complexity of light—Turner's sun smeared
in layers of darkness, thus he entered.   & Still's
      insistence to Pulverize the figurative residues!
thus he entered

into canvas where color was never enough & these
          grays in yellow = movement, never enough
or the modulation of blues in red + black
                              into Bach, not enough until
in the obliteration of memory we comprehend this
                                        discreet
ecstasy   this temple in which everything appears
invisible and vast
so the painting must be large, large enough to enter

into intimacy.
            You may enter. but you may not speak.

words have been written but he warned us against it:
          paralysis.   embalmment.   entombment.

            I take no sides he said, in this human
condition.   sacred or profane he said, they'll find it here.
   said also
      that we who weep before his paintings are sharing
                                                his experience
                                    religious experience
                                                of the painting

Art

In a time before this time
I bought a plane ticket and ascended through the sky
to Los Angeles for the day just to see some murals
from the cave temples of Dunhuang. The line was long
even with a time-ticket and they herded us mercilessly
through the reconstructed caves replicating the darkness
of the temples with barely a minute to see the paintings
but it was an experience worth seeking. And then
I ate some lunch because I like a small meal after art
and museum food is often pretty good, and wandered
in the various beauty which is the Getty until it was time
to get back to LAX and catch a plane north to home.
Who lives in the privilege to do such a thing? I did
in the time before this time. Despite anxiety
about the cost I flew Virgin Atlantic (in their violet
illumination of the cabin) to London just to see
some paintings by Rothko and that was more
than my money's worth as the capitalists say, a feast
in silence on abstraction. I'm running low on words
but to see requires no words, which is why to go alone
to art is so desirable and the particular wordlessness
within that solitude so glorious. *Silence* he said
is so accurate.

Once in a Blue Moon on All Hallow's Eve
at the end of a long Leap Year: a *stroke*, and to those
neural threads where in the *pons* perception, attention
and memory entangle by subtle means there was a wound
rendering the air a bright translucent dimensional density
of motion, the space before me jelly through which
I found my way slowly, distracted and absorbed
by every beauty even in the form and utility
of that green plastic hospital mug. To be absorbed
into beauty cannot be undesirable, nor can it be
unwise to learn from the snail, and anyway the time

for ascending on a whim into the sky, unmindful
of planetary consequences, is over for all of us.
Go slowly now, understanding the art of the snail
in her silver trail.

The neurologist advises
(looking straight into my eyes) to savor
life on two feet and recommends a book by Ram Dass
whose practice was love in helplessness—a profound
practice as the doctor pointed out although my thought
left unsaid was of those devotees who wheeled him
through the airports and museums. The actual
question for me now is not of possibility but of desire
and whether I might desire ever again to leave home
for art or for love or forever not to leave home
where with little dog I live in long tranquil mornings
and crickety nights and might enjoy that monkish life
which for me has always had both abstract and
emotional attractions. But what I know is that it's all
here, in the visible the tangible
and the intangible in this impermanent
placement on the ground called home
in this sufficiency of beauty and feeling
while I'm breathing

Painter Age Ten

Dylan

I understood
that house on fire, bordered black
somebody locked inside

and breathed again
into a wilderness of water & light
in two blue lines

or the shimmering
sun in a green bursting curve
your summer

and in that time
your narrow body bending, tuned
to what's essential

to the senses, discerning
the elements, body bearing light
as saffron robes

In Your Hands

for Izzi

One night when
a baby in your cot you awoke
into an inconsolable loneliness

your tiny hands, open & reaching
reaching up into the night

appeared as star-shapes
appeared as stars   and ever after

these two hands in the beauty
of their gracefulness, the certainty
of their usefulness

are always like the starlight
in which all life on earth was made

as you are a maker in metal
and clay, these earthly elements

And as you discover in movement the light
of comprehension, as the golden deer

appears & disappears silently
into the shadow glade

And oaring the boat
so confidently across the lake

And in my kitchen so kindly
washing the dishes

Frauentrost: Woodcut, 1920

for Alan and Paul

After the war, the cut—chisel & knife
into the grain. Into the cut
the battlefield.

Within the grain, the silence
of their intimacy—not softness
but the solace of endurance, of presence.

Into the woman's comfort that return
after war, and into his work
die stille Liebe.

Now in this room this moment from what
do tears arise? something here
in the grain the cut the touch

all of our losses, all limitation
and regret, all we left
unsaid & every

shattered soul in the bombed-out towns
every kiss, eyes closed every life
after war.

Gun Fire : *Palas por Pistolas* by Pedro Reyes

The city of Culiacán in western Mexico, long suffering
from death by gunfire, collected in trade for useful coupons
one thousand five hundred and twenty-seven guns

to be crushed in a public ceremony under a steamroller then
hauled away to a foundry to be melted into useful metal to make
one thousand five hundred and twenty-seven shovels

each handle engraved according to the artist's specifications to tell
this story. These shovels he delivered to public schools for planting
one thousand five hundred and twenty-seven trees

and in the artist's words the pedagogical purpose of this ritual
is to show how an agent of death can become an agent of life.
The shovels are beautiful.

Southern Exposure

Frankenthaler, thanks

In fifty-one colors intended
she said to be only beauty

(despite telling myself
& little dog who doesn't mind

that the day is only white noise
to which we dance a jerky jig

while above the birds that day
pours into itself as night, not

of the birds nor in the blue
nor even as some meditative

moment winding into itself
but only in the movement)

appears in that paint
what is

Oh this
place this hive
of embodiments, each
a bundle of senses, perception
in & out like air, unburdened
in breath
every sentience mysterious
to otherly bundled senses and yet
as it is

oh that song—
the mother & child reunion
is only a motion away
unbundled as light itself by just that
motion into reunion
as it is

oh this dog, herself
in the dog dream free
little feet on the dream run
sighs as we settle
resting together
in her spacious heart
tathata
as it is

Land of Enchantment

A flock of wild turkeys moved in this year
over on the laguna, almost always sedately
on the roam under the oaks. Yesterday
two frisky ones frolicked in circles
around the rest in what appeared to be
an effort to entice them into some fun.
No luck with the other fifteen turkeys
but witnessing their dance was my kind of fun
and enchanting.

Another enchantment: the marriage
of friends who live up Vine Street on the hill
and their daily celebration of easeful love
and beauty, with which they are generous.
In my heart see one at the piano, his hands
on the keys, and the other out back, his hands
shaping clay, or picture them sitting together
at the end of a day, with a bourbon. They appear
to have found their way through the years
into enchantment.

Today enchanted by this room,
just sitting in its shifting qualities
of presence as daylight changes direction—
in the perfection of the ceiling plaster
what workmanship, what mastery
of his art and in memory thirty years ago
my amazement at his gracefulness—
and the old Turkish kilim, this outburst
of color and angular form still and always
a shock to my judgment—and images, artifacts
each for its resonance, for its origins almost
an altar—and now in the animal comfort
of this easy chair at the window
warmed up for me by little dog.

It might properly be called a sitting room.
But for this chamber of my enchantment
the American term is surprisingly right.
                                        A living room.

Tide Pools

from Amanda

Her eyes always awake

see everything
and always have seen
since infancy this world
                    as works of art

and all the natural parts
        of this world
as her materials
for the work
        of making art,
        her practice
as a citizen of this world
        this fragile world
                    of beauty.

See her
out on the scarp
with her sketchbook,
                    herself
a work of art.
See her now on the mountain.

∞

Has made a field guide
to tide pools   of her love

for all the salty wonders to be found
at Schoolhouse Beach, and suddenly

it seems to me that I too am at work
on a field guide, in my case (as I am

old) a field guide to the inward life
which can be known now as tide pools

as a wild ocean tide ebbs out leaving
pools of liquid light where become visible

myriad forms containing the ways
of water and time.   memory.   time

Aquamarine

for Georgia, Oceanologist

In the glass dome at the aquarium
under aquamarine and brightness
and shining fish in motion, she jumped—
reaching   laughing   calling out
in ecstasy   *Alive! Alive!*— Georgia
three years old

in the ecstasy of her senses, into which
she entered so fully as life itself that
one day she said   contemplatively
I am not Georgia! which I understood
to mean *but so much more.* Or told me
some time later

examining a painting of the Kalachakra
I really like that map, how you go up
and up all the way here (pointing
to the center, which accurately describes
that mandala's dimensional expression
of the universe

and esoterically of time) her solemn
understanding a mystery to us but for her
only a child's unbounded awareness
unbidden and ten years on unwelcome
as the rattle of adolescence & pandemic
disruption

invade that exquisite sensibility
in its neurological complexity.
Such all-consuming mindfulness
now is painful.   requiring refuge.   requiring
the peace of deep ocean   calling her back
to aquamarine

The Living

Appears to begin
in respiration a varietal bio-
chemistry of transformation
in the complicated lichen, in water-
loving algae, in the ubiquitous bacteria
& in animals longing for oxygen lungs
breathing in breathing breathing out gills
for the oysters & fishes tracheae breathing
for the cockroach & here the damp fine skin
of your lover & this exquisite membrane
of the jellyfish all breathing
& fungi, like the animals
fond of oxygen, the penicillium & chanterelle
the velvety mold & the ancients encompassing acres
in the underground
& as plants wanting carbon
dioxide receptive to radiance & tuned
to movements of the moon for these
patient forms as phytoplankton bristlecones & roses
the cell itself will labor at respiration
Hear us
in your breathing—
the vast and comforting
we who live
& when it ceases we cease to be
what that was.

All Right

Everything is all right
he said. That *everything*
is all right the message delivered to me
from my cousin who visited on a whim
a psychic who told her someone
has a message, your uncle, the one
with a daughter has a message
for his daughter: that *everything*
is all right. And so the message

was delivered although she was
skeptical because my father was
dead for more than a year
and this cousin far away never
thought of him nor of me, and because
she went with a friend to the psychic
only as a lark. And I do not believe
in the endurance of personality
after death and surely not in the form
of psychic messages from the dead
although my grandmother
did receive letters from the dead
in what she called automatic writing
but my father, the psychic said, desired
only that I hear this reassurance

that everything is *all right*   even
that day, my mother wailing Don't go
No don't go & my urgency in his ear
Yes, you can go & with everything
else left unsaid in whirlwind around us
his hand emptied into mine and he did go.
And what I wanted was for everything
to be all right, that it be not chaos
nor my will nor the terror in her need.
And thus it is, in a moment which

might be that one, might be also
this one in the nature of time
as with the help of the Physicists
the Buddhists the Aboriginal people
we have come to understand it,
because forty years later *everything*
is all right upon awakening today
in the bright room, *all right* in the yellow
and in the blue and even in the unjust
and violent world unfurling always into
chaos, where still there might be stars
in a night sky, time to breathe a little
longer and for everybody for even just
one nanomoment in a lifetime to be offered
the news that *everything is all right*
and feel that.

I do not believe that personality
endures after death but as for my father
it seems he acquired there some power
to offer authoritative reassurance,
the last word so to speak, about my life-
long entanglement with worry and doubt,
an offering which in retrospect
in prospect of its usefulness was there
as an expansion of presence
in his soft hand in my hands, felt
as *yes*, and found its way back weirdly
through my cousin, and in the forms
and the colors I arrange within
the rooms in which I practice the art
of routine, and as the sky
is always changing.

And I suppose this is a prayer
that every being in the depth
of their suffering might even for one
nanomoment in a lifetime be offered
a night sky of stars and from my dead father
the news that *everything is all right*
and feel that.

Philosophy

1. Absence

The story
of somebody's death might begin *he was born*
at this time, in this place and flow forward
but according to Bergson *time* is an ineffable
and infinite *duration* in which the past
enters and interpenetrates the present, both past
and present an experiential reality. Let's call it
infinite nondirectional flow. Not clocktime, not
calendar time which is all about the movement
of bodies through space. Not a dimension
but maybe the infinite spaciousness, the energy
of pure awareness described by the Tibetans
as reality. I'm trying to say that *the past* in which
we lived together in this place *is present* as the infinite
duration of *his absence*, which is why death (someone
said) doesn't end a relationship but only changes
our experience of it. I'm trying to understand
that story.

2. The Simultaneity

At the far end of a silent search for acorns
of a certain shape, sat down in the sun
on a bench   and happened then
the tempered husk of hours fell away
into the silver-dark fly, legs in motion
lightly along these hairs on my arm, each hair
equally on fire, and the fly on fire.   Present
every gardener who labored here beginning
in 1953, bending, sweating, setting stone
nurturing these trees through their youth.
The artist present also who lifted her hand
to the wall of a cave in what we call France
and blew pigment to frame it. Present also
the moment when that hand appeared to me
and all apparent substance   in perfect   simplicity.
Present as well these ears to hear the bell
when it rang to bring us all inside for lunch.

3. Mathematics

Zero
is not, which is
why any number
            times zero
becomes (magic!)
zero — nonexistent
& likewise any number
                  times infinity
becomes infinite
& subject neither to arithmetic
nor my comprehension, but in effect
infinity & zero are the same, & what
we are, & how it is

John Cage

In the moment is where
some say we ought to live   in the quantum
particle we might perceive   as a moment
& this is right advice, because that   movement
past   into   future is anyway all   there is
an unnerving emptiness into which some enjoy
surrender   & some don't   dark energy (this is
physics   )   familiar   in music to those who hear it

as silence   Cage heard it   Miss Dickinson wrote
that   forever is composed   of nows,   leaving it to the composer
to Cage   to demonstrate

Medicinal Properties

Unable to concentrate—a diagnosis, he explained
of inattention unrelieved by medication—he turned

to the bebop masters of improvisation & in jazz, riding
each note into another   discovered attention

Likewise a candle, solo flame a wild improv
-isation with impetuous air, no stillness in it & yet

to something there the eye awakens in attention
as contemplation : chemistries

of sound & light devised by human intention
as freedom from bondage to distraction

In Music

from Stephon Alexander

This late longing to know
waves, not only oceans but all
vibrational motion
longing itself
as waves, beyond understanding & yet
some way knowable & now on radio waves at midnight

in a human voice hear that Pythagoras was not wrong
about the music of the spheres: gravity light sound all waves

a multiverse expanding & contracting an instrument
playing itself, this audible cosmology of resonance
every next note containing all possibility
for improvisation

Wonderful news!
in syncopated half-sleep
with Coltrane & Einstein in the groove

cycling harmonic & temporal riffs
quantum jazz, these waves an intimate ocean
of vibrational motion

On the Pacific await that earthquake, that tsunami
in which our bodies will comprehend a power
of waves & meanwhile
radio, an intelligent telephone, a magic oven.
the insistence of gravity. and as lately
in every living hour imminent arrival
into waves

Daily Report

Among friends a pledge to be wary
of too much news in the morning   in favor
of a hummingbird at the butterfly bush or the squirrel crew
terrorizing that little one stranded out on the end of a branch

or just the sound of silence until the neighborhood machinery
revs up to clear out dry leaves dead branches peeling paint
or whichever seasonal ritual is on for the day & to read
a poem, in the right words a compass for setting out
                    into the morning *routine*
                    from the French *route*
                    a road, a chosen path

Pandemic

Almighty life is happening here—

That rose, replanted, now nine feet high
Scarlet roses blazing in the sky

Poppies tall as the tough magnolia

Iris precisely the colors of a burning ember

Seven redwoods on the hill
still there! still there!

Forget-me-nots all over the yard
More always than the day before

And of course the squirrels

Deliverance

Merwin, thanks

Morning again, how it keeps on
arriving from the flux of night again
today as winter sun too bright for such
a cruel epoch beating now on the pages
of this book, perfectly bound, dispatched
to the ubiquitous old now in our garden
time gazing out however acutely old eyes
allow from a table at a window or a bench
behind the garbage bins into vistas opened
by your offering in language arriving
from the ocean where daily you labor
to deliver us into everything we know

Memoir, in Brief

Almost forever the experience
of sudden expression out loud
of something not previously
in my thoughts, not like talking
to myself but words apparently
unrelated to the moment, which
in my twenties most often were
Do you love me?
but fifty years later now it's always
I love you—both
apparently addressed to the many,
so as an indication of what's up
in the psyche this is movement
in a good direction.

These Days

My intention was in these days
to step gracefully outward, upward
into a galactic view of movement, not
to explain my   self   again. However
(announcing alternatives/contradictions)
instead it's often inward now & down
into low notes emanating from within
this body as though everything
                                        everything
poured into a vessel deep within my body
            no,   this body the vessel
like everything empty as a singing bowl
            which having been struck
            reverberates, sounding
sometimes like sorrow, sometimes joy.

Knowing nothing
has been my practice and always
I practice it. Becoming old
has been my practice and still
I practice it. The children
do daily practice
                                for a future

The Solitude

Beyond the problems of description

increasingly the reasons not to speak
outweigh the expectation for speech,
intimacy
now something undertaken as silence
in the grace of its absence
in the grace of its absence

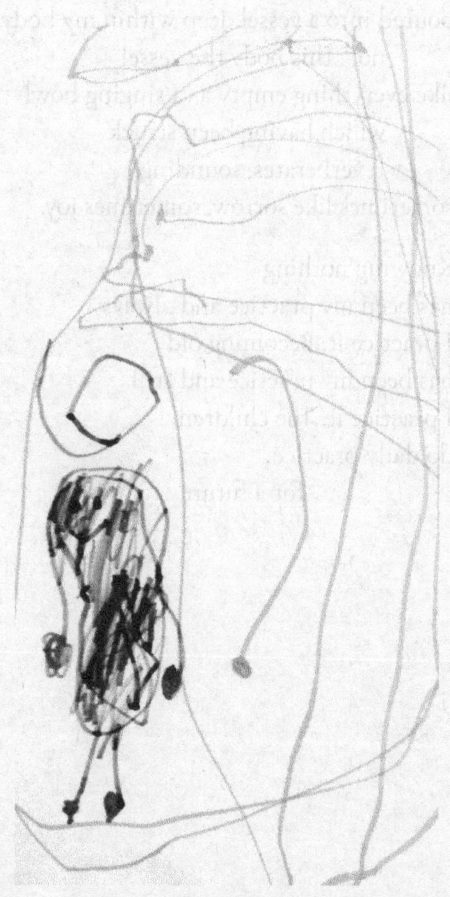

Drawing by Ruby Maxson.

In the Temple of Wind

ripples of cloud
across that blue—in the eyes

only air, everything now bending with it
                                        as in gratitude, all moved

into gratitude.   What earns devotion
                              won't hold it long, will shatter

as ripples of cloud   that blue the only
            purpose   the only temple
and bending together with these trees
                                                            is prayer

Written

Out from longing
that everything known or knowable might arise
without sound into music it comes. For bodies
unlike one another as species & alien in their form
their limbs their breathing their senses it arises
as longing. As longing to render known what we were
who were their ancestors into memory it comes.
As memory after this will recedes & after this breath
may it be known.

Title Index

N

O

P

Q

R

S

T

First Line Index

A

B

C

D

E

F

G

H

I

T

U

W